How to be a CANOEING STAR

by Kath Wright

British Canoe Union
Adbolton Lane, West Bridgford, Nottingham NG2 5AS

First published 1994

British Library Cataloguing in Publication Data.

A catalogue record for this book is available from the British Library.

ISBN 0 900082 05 4

Printed in Great Britain by:
Leicester Printers
164 Barkby Road, Leicester LE4 7LF

About the Author

Kath Wright first learned to canoe when she was 19 years old, and has participated in most forms of the sport. This has ranged from representing the North of England in sprint racing, to surfing; from touring around the Western Isles, to reaching division 2 in slalom.

For two and a half years Kath taught canoeing as a full time instructor at the East Barnby Outdoor Education Centre in North Yorkshire.

Kath now lives in Nottingham with her husband and two children. She has taught at the Colonel Frank Seely School, at Calverton, just outside the city, for seven years. During her time there Kath has introduced over 1,000 students to the 'pleasures of the paddle'.

ACKNOWLEDGEMENTS

I would like to record my sincere and grateful thanks to Malcolm Clough, Pete Coghill and Ian Hutchings for all of their helpful comments and suggestions when proof-reading my notes.

In particular I am indebted to Frank Goodman for his advice and for letting me so freely use his material on kayak and paddle design as printed in the BCU Canoeing Handbook and to Robin Goodliffe for his time and help on the paddle construction section.

Above everyone, however, I must thank my husband Andrew for his forbearance over the past two years when, hour after hour, I have hogged the use of our computer, for the innumerable times he has had to show me how to make it work and for all his help and advice at moments of crisis.

About the BCU

The British Canoe Union is the coming together of all who love that special kind of freedom which those enjoy who follow the path of the paddle.

The BCU seeks to ensure that our traditional freedoms are maintained and improved upon. That canoeing receives its fair share of attention, funds and resources. That those who wish to take up the sport are enabled to do so with safety and enjoyment, and with due regard to the rights of others and concern for the environment.

Formed in 1936, it is canoeing's national organisation and has over 17,000 individual members and 600 affiliated clubs. It's purpose - to unite everyone interested in canoeing and encourage others to join in the fun. It's aim - to provide a complete, specialist service - educational, informational, training expertise, improved access to our canoeable waters - thereby increasing the enjoyment, safety and skills of all paddlers at every level. Affiliated to the International Canoe Federation and the British Olympic Association it is the body responsible for national and international competition.

Information, advice, insurance, a licence to canoe on all 2,000 miles of British Waterways Board rivers and canals, a bi-monthly colour magazine, and an annual yearbook giving information on thousands of events and courses throughout the country, are just some of the benefits of membership

Why not support the cause, obtain the benefits, and contribute to the progress of this superb pastime, adventure pursuit, and sport, by joining the BCU, or its Association for Scotland, Wales or Northern Ireland?

Contents

Introduction

For those who follow the basic precepts, canoeing is a very safe activity. There is no need for anyone to expose themselves beyond the level of risk which they wish to take.

If paddling is confined to canals and simple rivers, enjoying the sheer delights of nature's highway, and a buoyancy aid is always worn, the risk of serious accident is virtually nil.

For those who seek thrills and excitement, however, canoeing has a great deal to offer. Whether it is in the form of surging shorewards on the face of a green-backed swell which has traversed a thousand miles of ocean, or riding the white water switch-back of a raging rapid, the 'adrenelin junkey' will find that the sport can more than satisfy their need.

Regardless of whether it is Olympic competition, or journeying on the sea, which provides ultimate fulfilment, you will need to have mastered, and then practised and applied, the basic skills of the sport. It is those essential building blocks for success which the Star Tests identify, and which this book is intended to guide you through.

It is strongly recommended that a course of instruction is undertaken, ideally through a club, or on a course, or an activity holiday. In that way you will be introduced safely and successfully to the sport, and will be able to identify the type of canoeing which you wish to pursue, before spending money on equipment.

For further reading, the Canoeing Handbook is recommended. Available from the BCU, it covers comprehensively every aspect of the sport, including safety factors and full definition of the basic skills.

About the Star Tests

The British Canoe Union's Star Tests were introduced in 1978. A gradual build-up of interest has occurred, and currently well over 20,000 tests are taken each year.

Their purpose is to provide a logical learning progression, and to act as indicators that a certain level of competence has been reached in the ability of the paddler to handle his or her kayak. The tests were never intended to be an end in themselves. They are meant as 'milestones' to confirm that an individual has reached an identifiable point in their journey to achieve their own full potential.

The aim of this booklet is to provide the Star Test candidate with the background information which is necessary in order to satisfy the requirement of the tests to ensure that paddlers are acquainted with, and are thus able to avoid, the potential pitfalls.

Geoff Good
Director of Coaching, BCU

ONE STAR TEST SYLLABUS

Aim: The test is designed as a basic assessment of ability at the end of a beginner's course. It is an 'encouragement' test.

THEORY (Each candidate to answer one question under each heading)
1. Capsize drill
2. Kayak, paddle and spraydeck
3. Personal dress and life jacket

PRACTICAL "A"
Each candidate must successfully perform each skill (but up to three tries are permissible).
1. Launch the kayak and get into it. *The boat must be afloat. Balance must be maintained. The paddle must remain within reach.*
2. Forward paddling over a circuit of at least 100 metres including controlled turns. *Some directional instability is likely to occur but this should not include complete loss of forward movement or a continuous careering from side to side.*
3. Paddling backward. *Turning the trunk and looking over the shoulder must be in evidence.*
4. Stopping in both directions. *Reverse motion should be in evidence after four strokes.*
5. Forward sweeping only to turn in a large circle. *The paddle blade should be covered. The paddler should reach out to full arm extension, elbow slightly bent, and draw well into the stern with the forward arm pushing across the body.*
6. Forward and reverse sweep strokes to turn 360 degrees in both directions. *The body should turn to place the paddle in at the stern of the kayak. A good full arm sweep must be in evidence.*
7. Return to the edge and disembark. *Correct approach for circumstances. Balance must be maintained.*
8. Capsize and swim ashore. *If a spraydeck is worn, it may be released before capsizing. Providing there is not total panic, the demonstration should be accepted. Failure to immediately hold and retain the kayak means disqualification. The paddle should be retained, or collected by swimming the boat to the paddle.*

PRACTICAL "B"

Demonstrate satisfactory beginning of:

1. Support stroke. *The kayak must be tilted sufficiently for water to reach the deck, but not necessarily to be off balance. A firm push and associated hip-flick to recover.*

2. Draw stroke. *The paddle blade to remain in the water. A push-pull action in evidence. Stern or bow swing acceptable. Paddle shaft probably not upright at the end of the stroke at this stage.*

3. Stern rudder. *With good forward movement of the boat, the paddle blade should be inserted on one side of the kayak, well back to the stern, and an attempt made to keep the boat running in a straight line with the paddle remaining on the same side of the kayak.*

ONE STAR THEORY

CAPSIZE DRILL

1. As soon as you realise that you are capsizing, bring your head to your knees.

   This tucked position is safer than leaning backwards with your face exposed to rocks or sharp objects beneath the surface. Also, if you lean back you won't be able to reach the grab loop on your spraydeck or be able to push against the kayak to slide it off your legs.

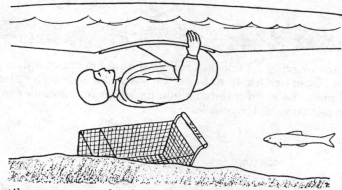

2. Wait until you are completely upside down, release your spraydeck (if wearing one), place your hands on the kayak either side of your hips, straighten your knees and then slide the kayak off your legs.

   If you try to kick the kayak off your legs you will just bruise yourself and take longer to come out.

3. Try to keep hold of your paddle and the cockpit edge whilst getting out.

   If you find that you have let them go then quickly:

   first – *grab your kayak before it is blown away from you by the wind or swept away by any river currents*

   then – *if possible, grab your paddle or swim your kayak to the paddle and grab it.*

   Keeping hold of your kayak is important because

   (a) your kayak will help keep you afloat,

   (b) your kayak is easier to see than your small head bobbing about in the water, and

   (c) you will be in the water less time than if your rescuer has to go in search of your kayak before emptying it and helping you back into it.

4. Leave your kayak upside down.

   Turning it over lets air out and water in and your rescuer will then take much longer to empty it.

5. In flat water, keep hold of the kayak and work your way to one end, preferably the front (bow) end, hang on to the toggle and tow the boat to the bank, or await rescue if in open water.

6. On river rapids, go to the upstream end, lie on your back facing down river and hold the kayak over one shoulder. Your feet should be the lowest part of you in the water.

   Adopting this position means that your feet and less sensitive areas (!) take the impact if you hit any submerged rocks or other obstructions, the kayak helps keep you afloat and, if the kayak does run into something solid, your arms will absorb the shock, not your teeth !

7. If you are wearing a lifejacket rather than a buoyancy aid, it should be inflated if you are likely to be in the water for some time. However, it should never be worn inflated when paddling so remember to deflate it as soon as you re-enter your kayak.

The Kayak

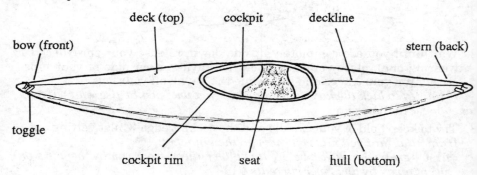

CHECKING A KAYAK

1. Check for holes.

   Check the top (deck), side seams and bottom (hull) for holes and rough edges. These can usually be temporarily mended with carpet tape.

2. Check the toggles, toggle ropes and decklines (if fitted).

   Check that there is a toggle at each end and that the toggle ropes and decklines are not frayed. Replace if frayed. Loops of rope instead of toggles can be dangerous in rough water. If the kayak is rolled over by the current your fingers may become trapped in the loop. Decklines should be taut.

3. Check the cockpit rim and seat.

   Check that the entire cockpit rim is securely attached to the kayak. If it is not then do not use a spraydeck on it. Check that the cockpit and seat have no cracks or rough edges. Temporarily mend any with carpet tape.

4. Check the buoyancy.

*Check that there is buoyancy **fixed** in each end. Polystyrene and polyethylene blocks should be fibreglassed in. If air bags are used they should be fully inflated and tied in. This is because in rough water the kayak will flex and any buoyancy which is just wedged in will quickly work loose and float out and away. A kayak without buoyancy in it will sink if it is filled with water. As a **minimum** each end needs sufficient buoyancy to float the kayak level (not more than 3 degrees from the horizontal) when a 6.5 kg lead weight is suspended at each end. Ideally a kayak should be packed full of buoyancy. Such a kayak will float high out of the water and tend to be carried around rocks by the current. One with minimum buoyancy in will float much lower when full of water and be more likely to wedge on rocks, collapse under the pressure of the water and break up.*

5. Do you need a footrest ?

*A footrest is not essential when on flat water, but it does make paddling more comfortable and more efficient. However, if you are going on fast or rough water, on the sea or surfing, a fail-safe footrest **must** be fitted so that if you collide with anything, eg a rock, you cannot slip off your seat down into the front of your kayak.*

THE PADDLE

The paddle blades are usually either flat or curved. Flat blades can be used by both left and right handed people. If the blades are curved, check the "feathering". To do this, stand the paddle upright with the bottom blade facing you.

right hand control

Now look at the top blade. If it faces to the right then it is a right hand control paddle. If it faces to the left then it is a left hand control paddle.

To check whether the paddle is the correct length for you, stand the paddle upright on the ground. With your heels on the ground you should be able to place the ends of your fingers over the top of the paddle.

Before using a paddle, check that the paddle blades are firmly located and that there are no rough edges to them.

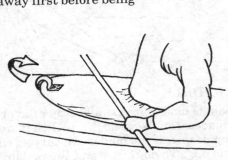

THE SPRAY DECK

Before using a spray deck:

1. check that it fits the kayak which you intend using ! They come in different sizes.

2. check that there is a grab loop/strap and that it is firmly attached to the spray deck.

3. check that there are no holes or tears in the material.

4. check that it fits comfortably around your middle. It should not be too slack otherwise water can get in and you might become tangled up in it when coming out of your kayak on capsizing.

5. practise releasing the spraydeck. Some end grab loops release easily on being pulled sideways, others release more easily if pushed away first before being pulled towards you.

LIFE JACKETS AND BUOYANCY AIDS

British Standards Institute Kitemark

Ideally a buoyancy aid should have "BCU/BACT Approved" printed on its label. Another good standard is provided by BMIF. Within the next few years, CEN (European Standard) devices will be the only ones available. However, not all of these would be considered ideal for canoeing.

A life jacket is only a life jacket if it conforms to British Standards 3595 and has the British Standards kitemark stamped on it. Technically it is only a buoyancy aid until it is fully inflated. BS 3595 will eventually be replaced by CEI5ON

A Lifejacket

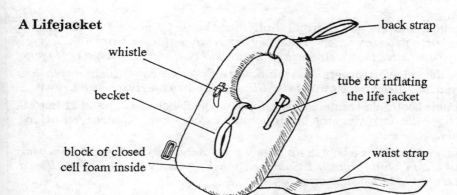

whistle

back strap

becket

tube for inflating
the life jacket

block of closed
cell foam inside

waist strap

Advantages of wearing a life jacket: If it is correctly fastened and inflated it will normally keep you floating face upwards even if you are unconscious. However, wearing a wet suit long john or trousers may make your legs so buoyant that the optimum performance is affected.

Disadvantages of wearing a life jacket: Lifejackets are more cumbersome to wear and do not provide all round body protection and insulation.

Buoyancy Aids

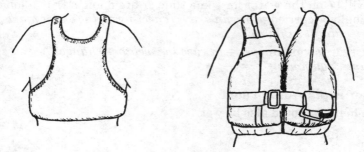

Advantages of wearing a buoyancy aid: It is easy to put on correctly. It gives more protection from the cold and from impact injuries to the back.

Disadvantages of wearing a buoyancy aid: If you are unconscious it will not necessarily turn you to float face upwards in the water.

WHAT TO WEAR

In cold weather:

a thermal vest – *if possible*

a wet suit long john – *if possible, otherwise trousers which drain dry quickly eg thermal trousers or tracksuit trousers,* **not jeans***. Trousers will not only keep you warm but also protect you from fibreglass rash if you are paddling a fibreglass kayak.*

woollen pullovers or a thermal (fluffy-lined) jacket – *when dry these trap a lot of air, a good insulator. When they get wet they quickly drain dry. Several layers are better than a single layer as air will be trapped between the layers.*

cagoule and overtrousers – *essential, not only for keeping rain and splashes off you, but also to stop the wind chilling you, particularly when you are wet.*

wet suit boots, old trainers or similar soft soled shoes which won't come off in the water or if you step out into mud – *stones and glass cut feet all too easily.*

woolly hat without a bobble – *a tremendous amount of heat is lost from your head if it is left unprotected. Some crash helmets can be adjusted to allow a woolly hat to be worn underneath.*

In hot weather:

trousers – *if you need to avoid fibreglass rash. Shorts, trunks or bathing costume are fine if a plastic kayak is being used.*

shoes – *to protect your feet.*

as little as you like on top !

BUT, always carry with you a cagoule – *to prevent wind chill if you do fall in. This should be tied into the kayak, eg to the seat, so it will not be lost if you capsize.*

If you will be on the water for some time or are doing a trip, a long-sleeved shirt should be carried – *the sun's rays reflecting off the water make for rapid and very painful sunburn.*

Also carry a warm pullover – *in case the weather changes or you spend too much time "swimming".*

On river rapids and in surf:

a crash helmet should also be worn.

TWO STAR TEST SYLLABUS

Aim: A test to be taken on a follow up course at a standard above beginner.

THEORY (Each candidate must answer two questions under each heading. Questions should relate to the paddler's experience – EITHER sea or inland).

1. Currents – tidal or river (show a simple knowledge)
2. Group control and signals
3. Effect of weather
4. Importance of personal ability

PRACTICAL "A"

Each candidate must satisfactorily perform each of the skills.

1. Support stroke. *Stationary and on the move, both high and low braces, performed on both sides. The water must reach the paddler's waist for high braces. A solid push with associated hip-flick should be in evidence.*

2. Draw stroke. *This should be performed on both sides. Top hand high, blade well covered. The boat must keep a straight line sideways through the water. The top hand should be pushing, the lower hand pulling. The blade is to remain underwater throughout.*

3. Low brace turn. *This should be performed on both sides. The kayak should be moving at a good speed. The turn should be induced by applying a sweep stroke on the opposite side. This is followed by a strong lean into the turn. The back of the paddle should be trailing on the surface ready for support.*

4. Capsize and rescue. *Capsize on the move – no setting of paddle or holding on to spraydeck on immersion. Letting go of the boat after surfacing means disqualification. The paddle should be retained throughout. The candidate must then be rescued from deep water and successfully re-enter the kayak. He or she must then rescue another paddler from deep water, putting them back into their kayak, with help if required.*

5. Good basic forward and backward paddling. *The candidate should demonstrate a dynamic seating position, correct width of paddle grip and correct entry and exit of the blade, with trunk rotation. There should be sufficient power in the stroke to paddle against wind or current and the paddler should be able to keep the boat running straight. When reversing, the paddler should look behind and unwind the trunk to produce power. The non-drive surface of the blade should be presented to the water.*

6. Stern rudder. *This should be performed on both sides. With forward movement of the kayak downstream or downwind, the paddle should be placed well back to the stern, blade upright. The kayak must be kept running on a straight course by the use of the paddle on one side only.*

PRACTICAL "B"

Demonstrate satisfactory beginnings in:

1. Sculling – support and draw. *These skills should be performed on both sides. A synchronised action should be demonstrated with the change of blade angle coinciding with the change of direction. The controlling wrist should perform the main part of the action. There should be a slight lean onto the scull for support (but the paddler need not necessarily be off balance). The paddle loom will probably be across the body for the sculling draw and the blade fairly high in the water.*

2. Eskimo rescue. *The paddler should demonstrate a recovery with lower body rotation from an upside down position whilst maintaining a hold on the rescuer's bow. Practise may precede the attempt until the recovery is from an upside down position.*

TWO STAR THEORY

GROUP CONTROL AND SIGNALS

Everyone in the party should be quite clear as to who the leader of the group is. The party as a whole should be close enough together for easy and effective communication between everyone but far enough apart that if one of the group gets into difficulty eg runs aground or becomes stuck in an unexpected stopper, the rest of the group doesn't follow suit.

The person at the front is responsible for setting a sensible pace so that the group stays together and no-one is left behind. Whenever there is the possibility of losing sight of any at the rear of the party, a "tail-end-Charlie" needs to be appointed. This person must make sure that no-one falls behind them. If necessary the "tail-end-Charlie" should be competent at rescue techniques.

It is usually a good idea to adopt a "buddy" system whereby paddlers organise themselves in pairs. Each paddler keeps an eye on his or her partner so that should one of them get into difficulties they are more likely to be immediately noticed.

Procedures in rapids
The leader must decide whether or not the rapid is safe to shoot.

If the rapid cannot be safely inspected from on the water, then the party should inspect it from the bank. If there is any doubt as to whether the group or any member of it can shoot it safely, then the rapid should be portaged (kayaks carried round it).

If the rapid is very easy or long, there are no rocks, trees, stoppers, or other hazards, which may pin or hold a paddler and the group is competent enough and just intend running the rapids without playing on them, then it is usually best to shoot the rapids with the paddlers in line one behind the other. Weaker paddlers should be sandwiched between more competent paddlers. Several boat lengths should be left between each kayak so that if one paddler does get into difficulties, eg runs aground or picks a poor route, the rest have enough time to alter course. Paddling a rapid too close together can lead to dangerous "pile-ups".

Signals must be agreed before setting off on the trip. One simple system is:

    hand jabbing in a given direction – go further over that way

    finger pointing, arm held out straight – go to where I am pointing and stay there

    hand or paddle held vertically in the air – stop, don't come down the river any further.

At points on rapids where paddlers may need help, a competent rescuer should shoot the rapid first and position themselves in an eddy where a rescue can be effected. The rest of the group wait in a safe position where they cannot be swept over the rapid. The paddlers should shoot the rapid one at a time, the rescuer below indicating when it is safe for the next paddler to set off. If the rescuer cannot be seen by the rest of the party then another competent paddler should be positioned close enough to the rapid (if necessary on the bank) so that he or she can see both the rest of the party and the rescuer below or that person's vertically held paddle.

Signals must be agreed before the rapid is shot. One system might be:
hand or paddle held vertically and still – stop, don't come down yet (in case
you need to stop someone who has already set off)
hand beckoning or paddle held vertically but moved with a circling motion
– the next paddler can proceed down now.

Procedures when surfing
Distinctive markers should be placed on the beach to mark the area within
which paddlers are to stay when surfing in towards the beach. These will
keep the group together and also prevent them being drifted along the coast
by wind and/or tidal currents.

If more than about four paddlers are surfing or there are several in the
group who are inexperienced, then it is wise to have a person as look out on
the beach in case anyone gets into difficulty.

A paddler surfing in has right of way over one paddling out. Surfers should
paddle back out outside the marked zone.

Cease surfing if swimmers approach. Explain the dangers to them and try to negotiate separate areas. In the event of two paddlers being on a collision course, they should both capsize. The drag of their bodies in the water will reduce the impact and the ends of the kayaks are less likely to impale vital body areas.

Procedures at sea

Generally when crossing open water as a group, experienced paddlers should be appointed to take the lead and the rear, and also with a large group, to take the left and right edges, so that the party is held together within a defined diamond.

On coastal cruises it is sometimes necessary to cross areas where surf intermittently breaks. This frequently occurs off headlands where shallow underwater ledges can run out for several hundreds of metres. If a group needs to cross such an area then they should go into "line astern" formation leaving several boat lengths between each other. Then if a wave does suddenly break on them they will be carried sideways towards the shore without the added danger of them colliding with any of the rest of the party.

Internationally recognized distress signals

Six prolonged blasts in quick succession on a whistle or with any sound or light device. Keep repeating the six blasts leaving a minute between each set of six.

SOS. Three short, three long then three short signals on any sound or light making device.

A red flare or an orange smoke flare.

Slowly and repeatedly raising and lowering your out-stretched arms on either side.

RIVER CURRENTS

Behind any obstruction, eg rock or tree, the river flow is interrupted and an eddy current forms which circulates the water back upstream. The stronger the main current, the stronger the eddy current.

If the obstruction stands up clear of the water's surface then the water will circulate as shown in diagram A on the next page.

If the water flows over the obstruction, the water passing over it will hit the water downstream and be deflected vertically upwards. Depending on the shape of the obstacle, standing waves or stoppers may be formed downstream of it (see diagram B). The peaks and troughs of standing waves stay in more or less the same position all the time and are often great fun to surf. Stoppers are generally formed after a vertical fall. The falling water makes a hole and causes the creation of a vertical re-circulation. For some distance below the stopper the water will be flowing upstream and downwards back into the stopper. Stoppers can be very difficult or even impossible to paddle out of and so are always to be treated with respect and should be avoided by anyone inexperienced.

Diagram A

Eddies
(from above)

eddy line (fence) where eddy current and main current meet.

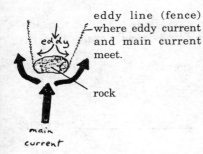

eddy line (fence) where eddy current and main current meet.

rock

Diagram B

Underwater Currents
(seen from the side)

river bed

STANDING WAVES - these hold their position though the water is moving on down-stream.

SURFACE STOPPERS form when water deflected upwards descends at a shallow angle into deeper water. A white cascading wave marks the position. Just below the surface, water is undisturbed

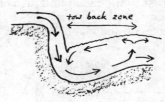

tow back zone

DEEP CIRCULATION STOPPERS are formed by water plunging steeply into a deep pool creating a long tow-back. They often occur on weirs Paddling straight through a stopper will involve paddling uphill against the tow back current.

Diagram C   TYPICAL RAPID

Diagram C   TYPICAL RAPID

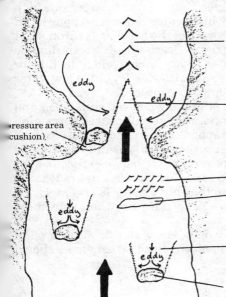

HAYSTACKS (pyramid shaped waves). These form below the point of the smooth tongue of water and are due to the eddy currents meeting, forcing the water upwards.

/\ - shaped tongue of smoother water - denotes where most of the water is flowing and therefore the safest route.

standing waves formed below

a submerged rock or rock ledge.

an eddy is recognised by the \/ - shaped area of disturbed water behind an obstruction.

rock

Haystacks are formed where two or more currents meet, as where the main current and the eddy currents interfere with each other pushing the water upwards in a series of pyramidal shaped waves (see diagram C).

Water hitting the upstream side of an exposed rock may be forced upwards to form a pressure area (often known as a cushion).

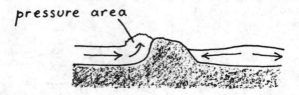

TIDAL STREAMS

The gravitational pull of the moon causes the sea levels to rise on the side of the earth nearest to the moon and also on the side directly opposite.

effect of the moon on sea levels – MUCH exaggerated !

Thus as the earth rotates on its axis, each place on the coast experiences two periods of high water in each 24 hours and in between there are two periods of low water. About six and a quarter hours elapse between one high water and the next low water, so each day high water is about an hour later. When planning a sea trip you need to be aware of the tide levels throughout the period that you will be out on the sea, eg at Scarborough North Bay the sea beats against the sea wall at high water so you must avoid launching or landing around that time. Also many bays and estuaries dry out at low water leaving vast expanses of sand, mud or worse to negotiate.

The sun also has a some gravitational effect so when the sun, moon and earth are in line, the sun's additional gravitational pull causes extra high high tides and extra low low tides. This happens twice a month just around new moon (no moon) and full moon. However the effect is usually delayed by a day or so. Tides at this time are called spring tides. In between these times, just after the half moon phases when the sun, moon and earth are least in line, the sun counters the moon's effect so that high water is less high and low water is correspondingly not so low. Neap tides are then said to be occurring.

In order for the sea level to rise in the North Sea, water floods in around the coast of Britain. The general direction of this flood stream is as shown here overleaf:

As the moon moves on, the water is drawn back towards the Atlantic. With only just over six hours to achieve this the water will be ebbing into the Atlantic on the west coast long before the flood stream has finished on the east side. Thus the time when the tides are at their highest will be different at different points along the coast, eg high water at Hull is about five hours after high water at Dover. Tide tables giving high water times and heights are obtainable from the Harbour Master's office, from newsagents or marine chandlers in the port nearest to the area you are going canoeing. Alternatively high water times can be calculated by finding the time for high water at Dover (available in many newspapers) and looking up the port in Reed's Nautical Almanac (or on tables available from the British Canoe Union) to see how much time needs to be added or subtracted to it. This time difference is known as the tidal constant for that port.

When the tidal streams are changing direction there is usually a period of "slack water" when the water does not appear to be flowing in any particular direction. The patterns of tidal flow around Britain are therefore fairly complex but nevertheless predictable. A typical "snapshot" of the directions of tidal flow around Britain is shown below. It should be noted that high and low water rarely coincide with slack water. At each point on thecoastcoast slack water and he coast slack water and high water will be separated by a set amount of time, though whether by minutes or hours depends on the location. Each location is different.

Tidal Streams Around Britain At High Water Montrose

During the six hours between periods of slack water the amount of water moving, and therefore the strength of the currents flowing, obeys the twelfths rule:

in the first hour – 1/12 of the tide flows
in the second hour – 2/12 of the tide flows
in the third hour – 3/12 of the tide flows
in the fourth hour – 3/12 of the tide flows
in the fifth hour – 2/12 of the tide flows
in the sixth hour – 1/12 of the tide flows

It can therefore be seen that the tidal currents are three times stronger in the third or fourth hours than in the first or sixth hours. On spring tides the maximum rate of flow will be considerably more than the maximum rates on neap tides.

27

Currents tend to be fastest between islands and off headlands as more water than normal has to be squeezed through. Where the effect is particularly pronounced it is called a tidal race. The water may be very rough especially if a strong wind is blowing or the wind is in the opposite direction to the tidal flow. A party of canoeists are likely to average only about two mph paddling speed so care must be taken to make crossings across such tidal races at slack water or when there is little current flowing, otherwise being swept out to sea becomes a real possibility. Alternatively, if you want most help to carry you down a straightforward section of coastline, you would choose to paddle during the third and fourth hours after slack water when the tide direction is favourable. Information about tidal stream directions and strengths is given on the admiralty chart or tidal stream atlas for that particular area.

The sea also behaves rather like a huge river with the shore as one of its banks. As with a river, back eddies are formed behind headlands and in bays. Where underwater ridges – often running out from headlands – and shallow areas – eg sandbanks – occur, the rough water produced is known as an overfall. Just like on a river, stoppers and standing waves may be formed which tail off into bouncy, confused water.

Besides the currents due to tidal action, localised currents may be created wherever there is wave action on a beach. Where waves are running in and breaking onto a sand or pebble beach, some water is carried forward and up the beach. This water has to flow back down into the sea. Steeply shelving beaches cause the waves to rear up and dump the water ("dumpers"). The returning water is most noticeable as a powerful undertow.

On less steeply shelving beaches the returning water tends to scour out preferred channels which allow the water to return as a fairly continuous and often powerful "rip" current. Rip current zones usually have less broken and smaller waves coming in over them.

Where there is a strong wave action into a bay then the rip currents frequently return the water via the edges of the bay.

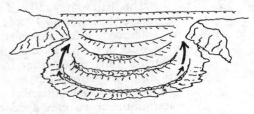

Thus rip currents can present a hazard. Swimmers, lilos and empty kayaks can all too rapidly be swept out to sea. However, they also sometimes offer an easier route out through the breakers for surfers. To escape from a rip current you obviously need to paddle out to the side of it, ie parallel to the shore, rather than trying to fight your way back against the flow.

River-mouths and estuaries also need to be treated with respect. The water flowing out from even a medium sized river may produce an outgoing current of confused water for hundreds of metres, with associated strong eddy currents for considerable distances to either side.

EFFECTS OF WEATHER

High pressure areas – "highs" or anticyclones – usually mean settled calm weather, but often they also bring sea fogs around our shores. They bring hot weather in summer and cold weather in winter. Low pressure areas – "lows" – usually mean cold, wet and often windy weather.

River levels are primarily determined by the amount of rain in the upper water catchment areas. It takes time for this water to flow down to where you may be paddling eg three days after heavy rain in Derbyshire, the River Trent will be high in Nottingham, 50 miles away.

In some areas close to a river's source, if there is little soil to absorb a downfall of rain then the water flows very quickly off the land, and sometimes a river can visibly be seen to rise – eg a rise of one metre or more in an hour is not uncommon on some stretches of the River Ure in North Yorkshire. When the river is very high it is said to be in spate. The water is typically very muddy and opaque from all the soil carried off the land. There is also a danger of fallen trees and other debris being carried along by the river. Trees which were growing at or near the water's edge may be partly submerged, with the danger for canoeists of becoming trapped – strained ! – in the branches. What might have been a nice gentle riffle may turn into a raging torrent with huge waves and stoppers and few bank-side eddies into which you can escape.

Running a river in spate is always a hazardous undertaking, even for experienced paddlers, and should be totally avoided by inexperienced paddlers.

Conversely, if there is an extended period of drought, some rivers may become too low or weedy for navigation and, particularly in lowland areas, the pollutants and toxins in the rivers become much more concentrated rendering capsizing inadvisable.

Prolonged hot dry weather and successive mild winters seem to be mainly to blame for the most recent problems of blue-green algae growth and "blooms" in many lakes and reservoirs. Where the presence of these blooms are confirmed, capsizing should be avoided as the toxins produced by these blooms are particularly nasty.

High winds can make paddling dangerous or even impossible. On the sea or larger lakes and reservoirs, if the wind is blowing off the shore then even moderate winds can make canoeing hazardous for the less experienced. With or without their occupants, kayaks can be blown away, making it difficult to keep a group together particularly if a capsize occurs. High winds also produce a severe chilling factor. Even on still waters like lakes, the waves generated by a high wind over a long fetch – the distance of clear water over which the wind passes – as on Rutland Water, can create large waves in a short time – see Table 1.

Table 1
The Beaufort Scale

Beaufort Number	General description	Sea	Canoeists' Criterion
0	Calm	Sea like mirror	Suitable for initial training from 'safe' beaches
1 1–3 knots	Light air	Ripples appear	
2 4–6 knots	Light breeze	Tiny waves. No breaking crests.	
3 7–10 knots	Gentle breeze	Small waves. Crests begin to form.	Life gets interesting for all. Good for practicing capsize drill. Getting tough for beginners.
4 11–16 knots	Moderate breeze	Medium waves building up. Some white horses.	About the limit for the proficiency test standard canoeist if on journey.
5 17–21 knots	Fresh breeze	Decidedly lumpy sea many white horses	Anybody over proficiency standard enjoys this. Usually creates very good surf.
6 22–27 knots	Strong breeze	Large waves everywhere. Continually white horses.	Short journeys by advanced canoeists alright, but you are reaching the border line.
7 28–33 knots	Near Gale	Sea piles up and spindrift off tops of waves	Surf tends to be big. Experts are beginning to swear.
8 34–40 knots	Gale	The difference from a landsman's view of these is difficult to	Surf gets to be very big, and you spend your time hanging on to
9 41–47 knots	Strong Gale	say except that the sea looks lumpy,	your tent
10 48–55 knots	Storm	high breaking waves and spindrift following wind path.	Surf enormous, and you get blown away with your tent.

When the wind is blowing in the same direction as the river or tidal current, then long rolling waves are created. When the wind is against the current, then a shorter, steeper chop is produced. At sea, a good force 5 wind against a tidal race off a headland may kick up a 2-3 metre high set of broken waves. Not a place for the inexperienced!

IMPORTANCE OF PERSONAL ABILITY

Basically, do not attempt anything for which you do not have the skills, experience or equipment, otherwise you are putting not only yourself but also possibly the rest of your party in danger.

Before setting off on a sea trip you should be confident paddling in continually bouncing waves and be able to surf, ie be able to brace sideways on a breaking wave and be able to use a stern rudder to control your kayak when riding a wave. Sea conditions are affected by a variety of factors, the main ones being: wind strength and direction, tidal strength and direction, swell (waves generated by the wind some distance away and which may be travelling in a direction contrary to the present wind) and the nature of the coastline and sea bed. When just one of these factors needs to be considered it is fairly straightforward to judge whether the abilities of the weakest member of the party match up to the conditions. However, when two or more of these factors come into play – eg wind against tide, or a heavy swell bouncing against steep cliffs or onto steeply shelving beaches – then the degree of difficulty of the trip is considerably increased. At sea anyone who cannot cope with the prevailing conditions is usually in serious trouble. On a river it may be possible for them to land and walk round a rapid they don't like the look of. Not so on the sea. You can be swept a long way in the wrong direction whilst being rescued; and exhaustion and hypothermia can quickly set in, even after just one swim. It is essential that the ability of the weakest member of the group is considered, as the group can only progress if he or she can.

Before setting off on any sort of river trip you should be able to control your boat on whatever rapids you are likely to meet. If, for example, a tree has unexpectedly fallen across the river ahead of you, or you see someone in front of you get into difficulties, you should be able to take avoiding action. A simplified version of the international river grading system appears in Table 2. It should be noted that the "skills" referred to for each grade represent the minimum level advisable before attempting to run the rapid "straight". A much higher skill level would be required before any success could be expected when playing on the rapid, eg: ferry gliding, breaking in and out, high crossing, and so forth.

Before attempting a rapid, be sure that at least one of your party is capable of rescuing you should you come to grief. Only attempt to rescue someone else if you have the skills to effect the rescue without yourself getting into difficulty – otherwise the eventual rescuer is faced with a far worse problem to sort out.

Canoeing is great fun, but always have respect for the water you are paddling on.

TAKE CARE !

THE INTERNATIONAL RIVER GRADING SYSTEM

Grade 1 Small rapids with regular small waves, regular currents and simple obstructions which can be easily avoided.

Skills: Ability to paddle forwards more or less under control, to turn and to stop.

Grade 2 The route through the rapid is straight forward though there are likely to be irregular waves, small stoppers, small pressure areas (cushions) and definite eddies.

Skills: Ability to paddle forwards maintaining control, to turn and to stop efficiently.

Grade 3 The route is recognisable but some manoeuvring is necessary to negotiate these larger rapids. High irregular waves, stoppers, strong eddies, isolated boulders, drops and other numerous obstructions are likely.

Skills: Good positive boat control, support strokes and the ability to ferryglide and break into and out of eddies and the main current.

Grade 4 The route is not always recognisable, inspection is usually necessary. The rapids are heavy and continuous with heavy stoppers, whirlpools and pressure areas (cushions).

Skills: Ability to execute the full repertoire of strokes efficiently (including rolling in heavy water) and to be able to link them together automatically as water conditions dictate.

Grade 5 Inspection is essential. Extreme rapids with narrow passages, steep gradients and drops with difficult access and landing.

Skills: As for Grade 4 but "par excellence".

Grade 6 Generally impossible without risk to life and limb.

Skills: For head cases only !

THREE STAR TEST SYLLABUS

Aim: When the candidate can pass this test he or she can consider themselves a canoeist rather than a beginner. The 4 and 5 Star tests are "advanced" awards.

THEORY (Each candidate must answer two questions under each heading)
1. Types of kayak
2. Types of paddle
3. Use of tow line
4. Personal equipment for a day on the water

PRACTICAL "A"
Each candidate must satisfactorily perform each of the following skills:
1. Sculling draw. *This must be performed on both sides. The paddle should be nearly upright and the blade deep. An effective sideways motion must be evident. The boat must be kept straight.*
2. Sculling support. *This must be demonstrated on both sides. The paddle should be low. The stroke should be performed with good solid sweeps and a confident committal to the paddle. The water must reach the paddler's waist and the kayak be off balance.*
3. Recovery strokes. *These must be performed on both sides, both stationary and on the move, and the strokes should be followed by forward paddling. The paddler should demonstrate good solid high support strokes with the kayak completely off balance (lower and upper gunnels in perpendicular plane).*
4. Draw stroke. *This should be demonstrated on both sides whilst on the move. The paddler should effectively pull the kayak sideways from its course without turning the boat.*
5. Bow rudder. *This should be performed on both sides. The paddler should demonstrate an effective turn around the paddle with the blade remaining forward of the cockpit.*
6. Eskimo rescue. *There should be a confident capsize and banging of the hull, with the rescuer moving in from 5 metres distance. A first time recovery must follow, but two attempts may be made. The rescuer should approach from in front of, or behind the paddler, to avoid risk to the rescuee's hands.*
7. Tilting the boat to assist turning. *This should be performed in both directions. The paddler should turn in a circle using basic forward paddling strokes (no sweeps) obtaining the turning moment by holding the kayak tilted on its gunnel.*

PRACTICAL "B"
Demonstrate satisfactory beginnings in:
1. Single handed rescue. *The paddler should demonstrate an effective lone rescue of another canoeist, returning him or her to their kayak in deep water. The capsized paddler may assist as instructed by the candidate.*
2. Eskimo roll. *The candidate must come up within three attempts, during each of which the instructor may guide the paddle, but not touch the boat or the paddler. A half roll is acceptable (ie down and up again on the same side).*

THREE STAR THEORY

TYPES OF KAYAK

Kayak, Canoe or Ski ?

All kayaks are canoes but not all canoes are kayaks !

Technically all kayaks are modified descendants of the original Eskimo (or more correctly, Inuit) hunting kayaks – ie craft which you sit inside and propel along with a double-bladed paddle. Canoes were the craft used by the North American Indians. Various tribes developed a wide range in types for different purposes from huge, war canoes to quite small, single handed ones. Both those and modern canoes are normally propelled using a single-bladed paddle from a sitting or kneeling position. In Britain, the term "canoe" has long been used for either a canoe or a kayak, but this practice is now gradually changing.

open canoe

A ski is basically a buoyant surfboard with shaped recesses for feet and rear. You sit on it and use a double-bladed kayak paddle to propel it.

Surf Ski

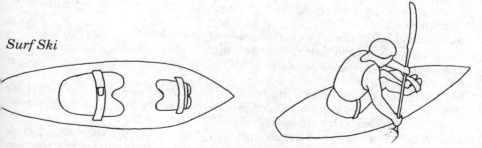

Shape and Performance

Specialised kayaks have been developed to meet the needs of each of the canoeing disciplines – eg slalom requires a kayak to be highly manoeuvrable, whereas a sprint racing kayak needs only to go fast in a straight line. Certain basic features produce known performance characteristics. For instance long waterline length – length of the kayak immersed in the water – gives high top speed. However, in many cases the desired performance characteristics may require conflicting design features – eg a slalom kayak has to be highly manoeuvrable when negotiating gates, and thus needs a short waterline length, but it should also be capable of reasonable speed between the gates. This calls for a long waterline length. Kayaks in competitions also often have to conform to design rules on length, width and curvature. Hence the resulting shape is inevitably a compromise. Though manufacturers keep trying to produce "better" compromises, the basic shapes of kayaks for each of the major disciplines generally conform to those shown below.

The Basic Shapes

Dimensions and weight for competition kayaks must conform to ICF (International Canoe Federation) Regulations.

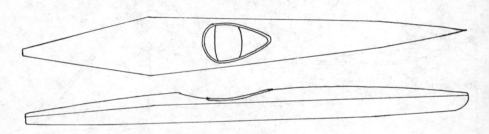

Wild Water Racing K1, 450cm(max) x 60cm(min), 10 kg(min)

Characteristics

long waterline length – for faster top speed
fine bows – to cleanly cleave through the water creating minimum disturbance
narrow and fairly semicircular in cross-section below the waterline – to give the minimum wetted surface to the hull, thereby reducing drag. The ICF minimum width regulations are achieved by extending the upper surface out to form "wings"
high volume, especially in the bow of the kayak – so that the bow lifts through waves. If the bow tended to plough deeply into oncoming waves much forward speed would be lost
widest part to the rear of the cockpit – so that the paddle can be placed as close as possible to the centre-line of the kayak. This reduces the turning effect of each paddle stroke giving more forward power
closed cockpit – the paddler needs to grip the kayak so that he or she can apply a force in any direction. This allows the paddler to lean, turn and roll the kayak efficiently as well as paddle it forwards.

36

Sprint and Marathon Racing

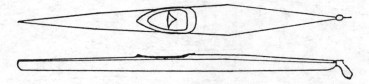

International Racing K1, 520cm(max) x 51cm(min), 12 kg (min)

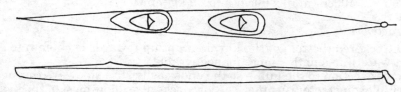

International Racing K2, 650cm(max) x 55cm(min), 18 kg (min)

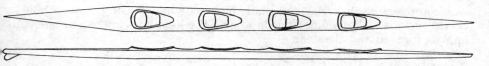

International Racing K4, 1100cm(max) x 60cm(min), 30 kg (min)

Characteristics

long waterline length – for faster top speed

fine bows – to cleanly cleave through the water creating minimum disturbance

narrow and nearly semicircular in cross-section – to give the minimum wetted surface to the hull, thereby reducing drag

forward cockpit position(s) – this causes the kayak to resist turning off course. The trailing part of the kayak acts rather like the long tail on a kite keeping it facing into the oncoming current

a rudder – so that you can turn when you do want to

widest part to the rear of the cockpit – so that the paddles can be placed as close as possible to the centre-line of the kayak. This reduces the turning effect of each stroke

open cockpit – to allow free movement of the legs. The forward propulsion from the paddle is most effectively transmitted to the kayak by the foot on the stroke side pushing on the footrest (though some racing paddlers prefer to push on the footrest on the non-stroke side as this reduces the turning effect on the boat). Pushing on the stroke side is, however, a much more natural action. The alternating paddle action gives rise to a "cycling" action with the legs.

Slalom K1

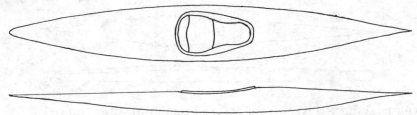

Slalom K1, 400cm(min) x 60cm(min), 9 kg (min)

Characteristics

much rockered (bottom of the kayak swept up towards each end) to give a short waterline length – more manoeuvrable

flat cross-section to the hull – so the ends easily slice sideways through the water allowing faster turning. The low decks also allow most of the kayak to pass under the slalom poles, so reducing the chance of the paddler incurring penalties

fine, low volume bow and stern – so that the ends cleanly cleave through the water and also so that they can easily be sunk when passing under a pole

closed cockpit – the paddler needs to grip the kayak so that he or she can apply a force in any direction.

Surf Ski

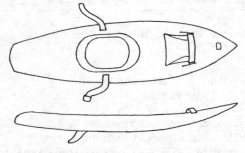

Most surf skis are between 215cm and 270cm long x about 60cm wide.

Characteristics

short and well rockered – for manoeuvrability

flat bottomed – so that it planes easily when surfing down a wave face

well defined rails (side edges) – less drag when planing down a wave, and also to prevent the kayak slipping sideways down the wave front. A fin is added to give even better grip. Hard edged rails also make the kayak sensitive to turning by leaning to one side or the other

rear seat position – to help keep the bows up particularly when surfing on a wave

surf board shape with only a recess for sitting in – so that it can be paddled like a normal kayak but has the behavioural characteristics of a surf board.

Sea Kayak

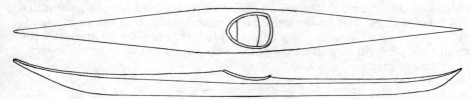

a "traditionally" shaped sea kayak

Most sea kayaks are about 500-570cm x 60cm.

Characteristics
long waterline – for faster speed
narrow, upswept bows – to resist sinking as the bows bury in a steep wave
the fineness of the bows keeps the windage to a minimum
round-bilged or chined hull shape – for stability in rough water

round-bilged   chined

bulkheads and hatches – to allow easy storage of expedition gear
low rear deck – when travelling, the kayak stern can skid sideways more
easily than the bow. Thus it is important that the stern deck, in particular,
is low to prevent the rear of the kayak being blown round when the wind is
from the side
closed cockpit – the paddler needs to grip the kayak so that he or she can
apply a force in any direction.
A shorter, more manoeuvrable alternative to the specialised sea kayak is
shown below.

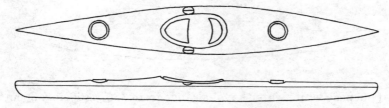

General Purpose Kayak

It is difficult to define the typical "general purpose" kayak except that it is
a kayak which can be used for a variety of purposes. By definition it is a
compromise between the various design features outlined for the preceding

kayaks. In the past many paddlers have used one of the "old-fashioned" high volume slalom kayaks. These can still readily be used for competing in at low level slalom, wild water racing and marathon racing competitions, for surfing and short, one-day sea trips and for river cruising. Obviously they would not perform as well as the various specialist kayaks would for each of their disciplines.

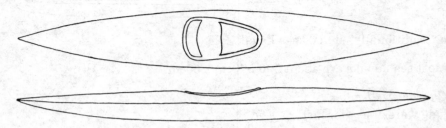

(400cm x 60cm)

Characteristics

moderate length – giving reasonable forward speed through the water
some rocker to the hull – for manoeuvrability
fairly large volume – to easily cope with rough water
round-bilged – for stability
closed cockpit – so the paddler can grip the kayak and move it in any direction.
More recently the shorter, plastic white water kayaks have become popular for flat and wild water non-competitive use.

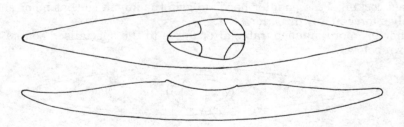

General purpose white water kayaks range from 330 – 360cm x 60cm

Characteristics

being made from polyethylene – very tough, fewer repairs
upswept ends – for manoeuvrability and to resist sinking in heavy water
blunt bows – safer for other river users and less likely to jam in between rocks

Placid Water Kayak/Touring Kayak

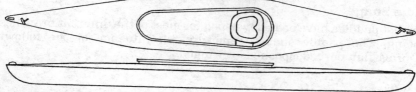

Touring Kayaks range from 400-500cm x 60cm

The majority of people introduced to canoeing may never want, or have the opportunity, to progress beyond paddling on flat water. Open cockpit kayaks capable of cruising easily in a straight line are often far more appropriate than the low volume, much rockered, closed cockpit kayaks designed for manoeuvring on rough water. Indeed many experience a real fear of being trapped in a closed cockpit kayak. David Train's "Placid Water Progression" was introduced in 1984 to meet these needs and to generally encourage canoeing on flat water.

Characteristics

long waterline length – so it travels in a straight line more easily and faster
flat bottomed – for stability
open cockpit – so that in the event of a capsize there is no fear of being trapped.

Baths Kayak

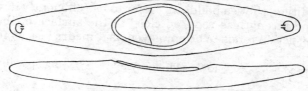

Most baths kayaks are between 183-274cm x 50-60cm

Kayaks used for Canoe Polo must have a maximum length of 300cm. Their width must be between a minimum of 50cm and a maximum of 60cm. Characteristics, such as the profile of the bow, must also conform to a number of other rules laid down by the National and International governing bodies for the sport.

Characteristics

short length – so that you can have a lot of them in a swimming pool at the same time
rockered hull – for manoeuvrability
round-bilged – for stability and ease of rolling
closed cockpit – the paddler needs to grip the kayak so that he or she can apply a force in any direction
blunt, rounded ends (bows and sterns) – so that they are less likely to cause impact damage to other kayaks, pool tiles or paddlers.

TYPES OF PADDLE
Paddle Shape

Specialist paddles have been developed for most of the different branches of canoeing. The paddle shapes generally fall into one of the following categories: flat, curved, spooned, or winged.

Flat Blades

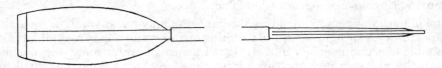

Beginners often use this sort as their performance is fairly predictable. They are also popular with canoeists who enjoy just playing around in rough water, eg Squirt boat paddlers, as the flat blade allows both surfaces to be used with equal efficiency.

Many sea canoeists use a long, narrow, flat blade similar in shape to that originally used by the Eskimos. The increased length of the blade gives it about the same blade area as other paddles and hence about the same amount of power can be applied to the water. However, the longer paddle makes for a longer stroke and one where the force is more gradually applied to the water. This makes paddling much less strenuous.

In addition, the sea paddle is easier to use efficiently in windy conditions. The wind strength is reduced close to the surface of the water so a low paddling action tends to be employed as it incurs less wind resistance.

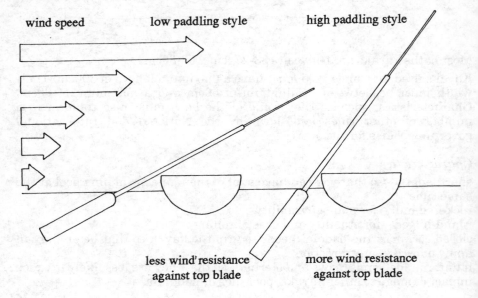

When paddling with a low action, it is easier to keep the blade of a long narrow sea paddle completely immersed than it is a wider, general purpose blade.

General purpose type of blade tends to break the surface and therefore be less efficient

Narrow blade is totally immersed

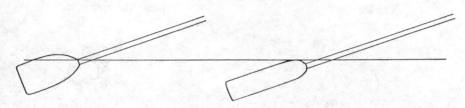

Curved Blades

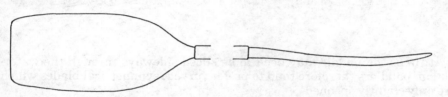

This sort of blade is often favoured by paddlers who want speed through the water and also the ability to manoeuvre their craft in rough water. This is the type used by many white water and slalom paddlers.

Spooned Blades (sometimes symmetric in shape but more usually asymmetric)

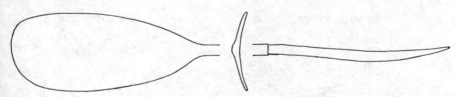

Sprint racing, marathon racing and whitewater racing competitors are only really interested in a paddle which performs well when paddling forwards, ie one which will grip the water well during forward paddling. Given blades of the same width and length, a spooned blade has a greater surface area for gripping the water than either a flat blade or a curved blade. In effect, its cupped shape better "holds" the water in place during the pulling phase of the stroke, whereas the water slips off the edges of the other two shapes more easily.

For the blade to cleanly enter the water, the end of the blade needs to be shaped so that it is parallel to the surface during the stroke. Normally one corner of a "square" ended blade enters first. This problem is overcome by the asymmetric shape of most racing blades. On the other hand, a slalom paddler needs a paddle which will give him not only good forward speed, but also perform well in a variety of other ways, eg in an upright manner – as in a draw stroke, and when the drive face of the blade faces forwards – as in a bow rudder.

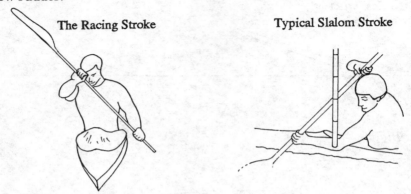

The Racing Stroke

Typical Slalom Stroke

At times the paddle may need to be sliced sideways through the water. Slalom paddlers therefore tend to prefer curved, symmetrical blades which are only slightly spooned.

During the entry phase of the forward paddling stroke, a curved blade not only wastes less energy but also generates forward movement of the blade itself. This occurs to an even greater extent with an asymmetric blade. Air flow over the aerofoil shape of an aeroplane wing generates a lift force which keeps the aeroplane in the air. Similarly, as the blade is sliced down into the water, the forces generated cause the blade to move forward in the water.

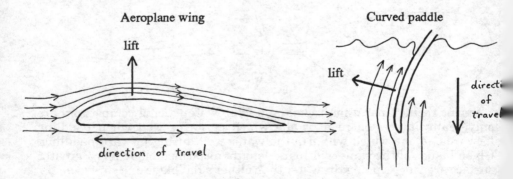

Aeroplane wing

lift

direction of travel

Curved paddle

lift

direction of travel

A flat blade, however, will tend to carry air into the water with it causing turbulence around the back of the blade. This is similar to what happens when an aeroplane wing meets the oncoming air at too steep an angle, ie it stalls and no lift is generated.

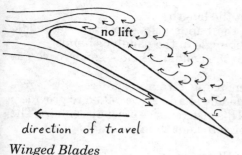

aeroplane wing in a stalled attitude

no lift

direction of travel

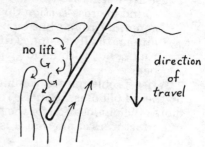

turbulence on back of flat blade
generates little forward force

no lift

direction
of
travel

Winged Blades

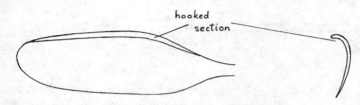

hooked section

This "high tech" shape was first used in international racing in 1985. From side to side it is aerofoil-shaped with the leading edge of the aerofoil on the outside of the blade. As the blade is pulled back and outwards from the kayak it generates a little more forward lift than the other blade shapes. However, using it to its full potential requires a special and very precise technique. It is mainly used by racing paddlers.

Paddle path when using a winged paddle blade

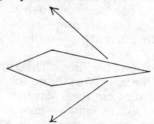

Feathering

Paddles are normally "feathered", ie the blades are set at different angles to each other. This helps to reduce resistance as the blade is recovered through the air and achieves a better position for the wrists, The majority of paddles in general use have blades set at 90 degrees to each other. However, many paddlers now use other settings: wing blades are normally set at 60-75 degrees, sea paddles are usually at 80 degrees and asymmetric paddles are commonly set at 83 degrees. Tenosynovitus – an inflammation of the wrist fairly common among canoeists – can be alleviated by an adjustment of the angle of "feather".

Shafts

These are normally either:
- round in cross-section throughout the length
- generally round but oval where the hands grip – so that the paddle automatically assumes the correct angle in the paddler's hands
- round, but with hand grips where the paddle is held – same reason as before.

Wrist problems are common when using straight shafted, 90 degree feathered paddles. "Double-Torque" paddle shafts are cranked to provide a more efficient location for the hands. This also reduces wrist discomfort. The manufacturers claim that it is 5% more efficient than a straight shaft.

The "Double-Torque" Cranked Paddle Shaft

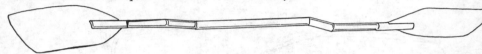

Materials

Wood. Some of the cheapest flat and curved blades are made from marine ply. These are fixed into alloy shafts. Laminated blades tend to be expensive but perform well, and the types with integral wood shafts are very comfortable to use, eg Kober, Azzali.

Glassfibre. In the past these were laid up by hand. The gel coat was brushed onto the mould then layers of fibreglass mat and resin were added. Nowadays there are a variety of constructions incorporating fibreglass, eg injection moulding (where fibreglass matting is sandwiched between layers of gel coat and then the resin is injected). Several manufacturers use foam inserts with a fibreglass finish, eg Paddle Sport, Kober and Schlegel. All these paddles tend to be rather expensive.

Plastic. ABS injected and polypropylene injected paddles can be produced very cheaply and are currently manufactured by Ace and Pyranha, among others.

RIM (Reaction Injection Moulding). This construction involves the injection under pressure of foam polyurethane (car bumper material). Sometimes alloy rim strengtheners are incorporated. The paddles produced are very strong but are not as lightweight as those made out of fibreglass and so tend to be used most on heavy whitewater. Such paddles are produced by Ainsworth (New Wave) in the UK, by Moll in Germany and by Perception in the USA.

The cheapest shafts are made out of alloy and the mid-range models from a high grade alloy. Alloy shafts have little flexibility compared to fibreglass ones. Stiff shafts are usually preferred for the shorter sprint events, ie 500m and 1000m, but they tend to jar the muscles and muscle insertions and so a more flexible shaft is normally preferred by other paddlers. Carbonfibre fibreglass shafts are much lighter and stronger, weight for weight, than ordinary fibreglass so, though expensive, are preferred for racing.

USE OF TOW LINE

On even the best organised trips things occasionally go wrong, eg the force 4 head wind that springs up from nowhere, the incapacitating tummy bug, the kayak that for once was not hung on to following a capsize. A good tow line is essential for dealing with these and other situations.

Before leaping in to rescue the tired, the sick and the flotsam, always bear the following principles in mind:

1. safeguard yourself. *Make sure that you are not putting yourself in undue danger. If you become a casualty then the situation is at least twice as bad for the next rescuer to try to sort out. At worst let there be just one lost, not one plus a foolhardy hero.*
2. safeguard the rest of your group. *Then, with any luck, you will just have the one rescue to perform at a time.*
3. consider how best to go about the rescue. *When rescuing a person or kayak, do you need to attach the tow immediately or would it be better to let it float through to calmer water ?*

As a general rule only use your tow line if:

1. that is the only quick way of affecting the rescue. *– instead could you push the capsized kayak to the bank using the bow of your kayak? With a sick or injured paddler would it be wiser for them to walk along the river bank ?*
2. you are confident that you can handle towing in the prevailing conditions

3. you are sure that by setting up a tow you are not putting yourself and/or the person being towed in danger, *eg by trying to tow when there is a risk of you being swept over a weir or down a severe rapid, or there is danger of you or the person / kayak being towed running aground, being pinned against rocks, or the rope becoming snagged on overhanging trees, and so forth.*
4. you know that you can cope with anything unforeseen lurking ahead out of sight round the next bend – *imagine confronting the branches of a fallen tree that is blocking the river ! In dubious situations you may need to have another paddler scouting ahead to ensure that all is well.*
5. the person being towed can cope with the tow – *ie he or she can keep their kayak running straight, or another paddler is available to support them. The danger is that as the towed kayak veers to the side the sideways pull of the line will tend to capsize them.*

47

WHAT WOULD
YOU
DO?

Whatever towline system you use it must be possible to:
1. secure it in seconds – strong winds and /or current can soon sweep you away into more difficult water
2. secure it with one hand – so that the other is free to hold the kayak or body to be towed. It's embarrassing having to recapture your victim if you let go !
3. stow it quickly and securely after use – preferably without needing aid from anyone else, in case they are not around to help you. A trailing line will all too easily snag or tangle around you with possibly dire consequences. Similarly, it must not be possible for it to accidentally come loose when paddling, capsized or swimming. The Suzy tow line has a velcro fastened pouch into which the tightly coiled line is stuffed. If the pocket on an expedition type of buoyancy aid is used, then the line tends to gradually pull out. This can be overcome by attaching a rubber bung to the line where it sits just inside the pocket
4. quickly release the tow from your end, even when under considerable tension – another paddler in trouble, a wave about to "mangle" you, or the towed kayak lodged. It is easy to conjure up all kinds of situations where you must get rid of the tow . . . and fast !

5. tow two or more kayaks – if a paddler becomes ill or injured, then that person may need the physical and mental support of another canoeist. This is most easily done by clipping together the bows of the two kayaks

48

which are to be towed. Two kayaks towed in this manner tend to veer from side to side far less than a single kayak, and so provide a much more stable ride.

6. vary the length of the towing line – if no-one else is available to support an injured/ill paddler, then he or she will have to use your own rear deck as a support. In this situation you need a very short tow line. If you have a front deckline it may be best to tie the towline to it with a slip knot (for quick release) so that the patient rests on your rear deck immediately behind you. Alternatively, you may find yourself towing in steep waves. Then you need some distance between your kayak and the one you are towing, if you are to avoid that crunching sensation as your kayak slows on climbing the wave in front, and the towed kayak accelerates down the wave behind !

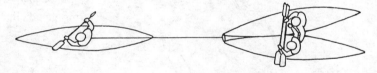

7. immediately pick it up off the water if you drop it ! – therefore use a line which floats and, if you use a metal spring-gated clip (stainless steel so it does not rust) run that end of the line through a float buoyant enough to support the clip.

Many inland paddlers prefer to use a tow line attached to their waist. This leaves the kayak deck clear of obstructions which might snag on overhanging branches, or other obstructions. Towing from the waist puts less strain on the back than an "over the shoulder" type. Also, the waist attachment point allows the person towing, freedom to manoeuvre his/her kayak independent of the kayak being towed – an important consideration when trying to tow a kayak into an eddy. A fail-safe release system is vital, however – there must be no chance of "taking a swim" down a rapid with a tow line trailing from one's waist. The majority of tows on inland rivers tend to be for a short distance in rough water. Tows over a longer distance would be on flat water. Therefore, for most of the situations which arise on inland rivers, towing from the waist should not put an undue strain on the person towing, so long as a broad waistband is used to spread the load. It also helps to include a loop of thick shock cord in the system to take some of the shock loading off the person towing. It is wise to knot the shock cord into two loops in the rope so that should the shock cord snap (it does have a limited life !) you retain your captive audience.

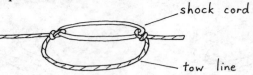

You can purchase ready made tow lines or make your own. One possible version might be as below.

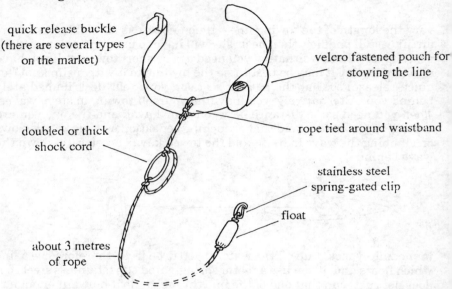

quick release buckle
(there are several types
on the market)

velcro fastened pouch for
stowing the line

doubled or thick
shock cord

rope tied around waistband

stainless steel
spring-gated clip

float

about 3 metres
of rope

Towing at sea invariably seems to involve towing for a considerable time, often in less than calm conditions. Towing from the waist is far too stressful and should be avoided. In order to tow a kayak in as straight a line as possible it is best for the point of attachment of the towing boat to be as close as possible to the kayak being towed. This can be achieved by passing the tow line through a loop at the stern of the kayak (not the toggle loop as it will slowly be chafed by the action of the line). Then, so long as there is enough line to avoid bumping in wave troughs as previously described, the towed kayak should not veer about so much. The system thus described works well when a sea kayak is doing the towing. A white water kayak tends to be slewed around too much as the towed kayak veers from side to side. In this case it is better to take the line through a small detachable loop which rests around the kayak's stern. On attaching the tow line, this loop will slip off the stern so that the towing point is from just behind the cockpit. With either system it is easier to have both the clip end of the rope and the free end of the rope (usually fastened off through a cleat) to the side and behind the cockpit. One possible system is shown below. For clarity the rope is drawn much looser than it would be when in use.

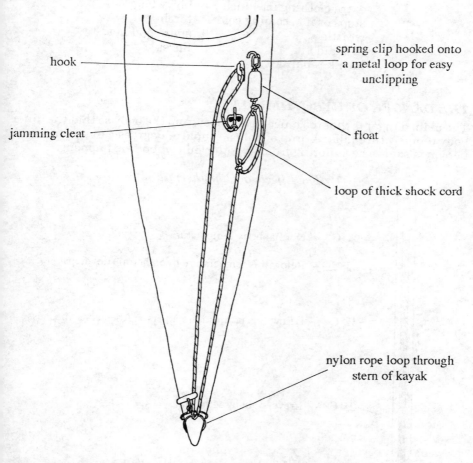

hook

spring clip hooked onto a metal loop for easy unclipping

jamming cleat

float

loop of thick shock cord

nylon rope loop through stern of kayak

When the spring clip is disconnected from the metal loop, the spring clip is behind the cockpit. This is an awkward position from which to try to attach it to another kayak. When the rope is released from around the hook, it allows the spring clip to be brought forward to level with the paddler – a much easier position to work from.

PERSONAL EQUIPMENT FOR A DAY ON THE WATER

CHECKLIST: appropriate clothing
helmet?
extra clothing for lunch
stops or if becoming cold
whistle
first aid kit
kayak repair kit

food and drink
waterproof containers
bivvy bag ?
torch ?
spare paddles ?
flares ?

THE DANGER OF HYPOTHERMIA

The main danger is that too much heat is lost from the body so that the inner body temperature falls. A drop of only a couple of degrees can be serious. A person is said to be suffering from hypothermia when this happens.

The Effects of Hypothermia

37°C --- Normal body temperature

35°C --- Below this temperature hypothermia develops

32°C --- Below this temperature a person loses consciousness

25°C --- Irreversible hypothermia

A person starting to be affected may show one or more of the following signs
unusual or erratic behaviour
yawning and/or complaining of feeling tired and very cold
speech becoming slurred
the person is very cold to the touch
co-ordination becoming poor
uncontrollable shivering

52

As the body's temperature drops still further the person may lose consciousness.

As soon as hypothermia is suspected, the person should come off the water – continuing paddling will only deplete that person's energy reserves still further. He or she should be immediately protected from the wind. A bivvy bag can become a temporary cloak or the person can crawl into it. If possible, the person should be quickly helped into dry warm clothing or at least have extra insulating clothing wrapped around them. He or she should then allowed to rest well protected from the wind and elements inside the bivvy bag. If necessary, another dry and warm member of the party should cuddle up with the casualty to provide extra warmth.

Warm sweet drinks can be given if the casualty is conscious but on no account should any alcohol be given. Alcohol will cause the blood to circulate to the body's surface where it will be chilled by the cold flesh. When the blood returns to the body's core it will reduce the body temperature still further.

Even after the person has apparently recovered they should not exert themselves and should stay well protected from the cold as their body's temperature regulating mechanism will have been affected and they are likely to be very susceptible to hypothermia for some time, probably days. If a support party is near they should come off the water for at least the rest of the day for mild cases. It is essential to seek medical advise after a more serious case. If it is impossible to evacuate by land then it is worth considering towing the person, preferably as a double tow to provide physical and psychological support to the victim. The partner is also then easily able to keep a wary eye on the person in case signs or symptoms of hypothermia reappear.

Whenever one member of a party is suffering from hypothermia, then, unless they are the only one to have capsized, it is safest to assume that the rest of the party may be starting to suffer as well. Every effort should be made to keep the whole group warm and in good spirits. The plan for the rest of the day should be carefully reviewed before proceeding.

Appropriate Clothing

For summer and relatively mild conditions, the notes on "What to Wear" in the One Star section apply.

When considering full day sessions during the winter, or on very cold rivers or the sea, then more serious consideration must be given to what is worn. If inadequate clothing is worn there is a serious risk that hypothermia will set in.

There are essentially three alternatives which can, to some extent, be mixed and matched:

Thermal Garments

Ideally a long-sleeved thermal top and tights made from tightly knit synthetic fibres are worn next to the skin. This type of material traps body heat but allows sweat to evaporate. It also very quickly drains dry after a swim. Over them are worn thermal pile (fluffy-lined) jackets and trousers. Several layers are better than one single thick layer, as air is then trapped between the layers. As air is a good insulator, the more air that is trapped, the better the insulation. A cagoule and overtrousers must be worn for protection from wind and water.

On rivers, wearing a cagoule with a hood is inadvisable as there is always the risk of the hood snagging on overhanging branches. On the sea, a cagoule hood is desirable as it protects both the head and the neck from the wind and cold. However, a hood inevitably reduces the wearer's sense of hearing.

Advantages: very comfortable and the amount worn can be varied to suit changing weather conditions. Drains dry on you and quickly regains most of its insulating properties.

Disadvantages: gives inadequate protection from the cold during prolonged immersion.

Wetsuit Garments

These vary from just thigh-length shorts, to full, single-piece suits with arms and legs. They also come in a variety of thicknesses and finishes.

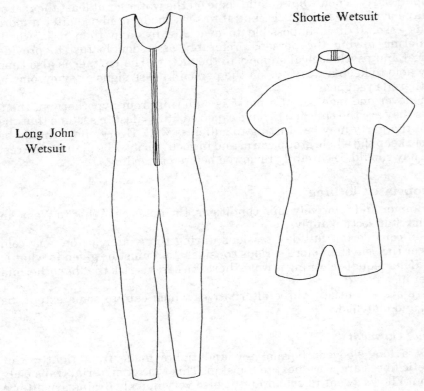

Shortie Wetsuit

Long John
Wetsuit

The neoprene, from which wetsuits are made, is in itself is a good insulator. Generally, the thicker the neoprene, the more insulation it provides. In addition, if you do become wet, any water trapped between you and the wetsuit also acts as a good insulator. However, any water draining out will carry with it vital body heat. Therefore the wetsuit should be close fitting to ensure very little change in the water next to the body.

Though modern wetsuit materials are fairly stretchy, most paddlers prefer to wear armless "long johns" or "shorties" as repeatedly flexing the wetsuit arms when paddling can be very tiring. It can also lead to sores where the material rubs, especially when paddling on salt water.

Wetsuits with unlined outer surfaces have been known to stick fast to kayak seats (!) so it is advisable to wear an old pair of trousers over them. The trousers will also protect the neoprene from snagging on rough surfaces.

Wetsuit bootees and boots are particularly useful for keeping the feet warm. They must have good soles or shoes should be worn over them so that your feet are protected from rocks and sharp objects. Wetsuit balaclavas can be very effective when capsizes are likely. Unfortunately some types tend to reduce your sense of hearing.

Advantages: good insulation during prolonged immersion and good physical protection from impact.

Disadvantages: can be very uncomfortable if worn for long periods or in hot weather. Extra warmth can be gained by wearing a thermal vest underneath and a cagoule over the top, but apart from these measures it is difficult to quickly or greatly modify what you are wearing if the weather conditions change.

Drycags / Drysuits

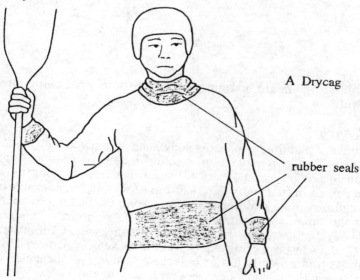

A Drycag

rubber seals

Drycags have thin latex rubber seals at the neck and wrists which prevent water entering when paddling, although in a prolonged swim some water will tend to work its way in. Drysuits come as either separate tops and bottoms, or as one-piece suits, and are totally waterproof. Some condensation is bound to occur as you sweat, but use of thermal vests/tights and thermal pile jackets/trousers ensures that the sweat is carried away from the skin and is not uncomfortable.

Advantages: comfortable to wear and provide effective insulation whether in or out of the water.

Disadvantages: because it provides such effective insulation there is a tendency to overheat if the sun comes out or you are working hard. A light coloured top absorbs less radiant heat and so reduces the likelihood of overheating in strong sunshine.

Helmet

A helmet should be worn when paddling on river rapids, in surf or when canoeing at sea near rocks, eg shallow areas, caves or cliffs.

The helmet must be adjusted to a snug fit so that it sits low on the head to protect the forehead, and cannot slop around and expose the side of the head, or temple. It should incorporate a shock absorbing foam liner.

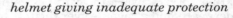

helmet worn correctly   *helmet giving inadequate protection*

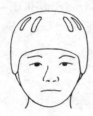 

The chin-strap should be tight to prevent the helmet being forced off in violent water.

Extra Clothing

The exercise of paddling generates body heat. When you stop, eg for a lunch break, you will quickly cool down in cold weather. As soon as you stop it is advisable to put on extra layers to retain body heat. Lengthy swims or frequent rolling in cold water can result in rapid and considerable body heat loss. The unfortunate paddler may be too cold, too lacking in energy or too timid of the rough water to be able to paddle vigorously enough to raise his/her body temperature. In all these instances heat retention is most effectively done by protecting exposed skin. This can be achieved by donning gloves/mitts and a woolly hat or balaclava. Taking off a cagoule to put on another thermal top may be necessary, but it can cause you to lose a considerable amount of body heat. An alternative is to put on an extra, lightweight cagoule over the top of everything, including your buoyancy aid. This will trap a layer of air which acts as an effective insulator.

Extra clothing carried in the kayak should ideally be of the thermal pile type so that should it subsequently become wet it will still keep you warm.

Whistle

This needs to be loud, plastic (so non-rusting) "pea-less" and attached to you so that it can:

> be used immediately
>
> be used whilst still attached to you
>
> be tucked securely out of the way so that it cannot swing up and poke you in the eye.

The international distress signal is six prolonged blasts repeated at 1 minute intervals.

First Aid Kit

As a general guideline, only carry items which you know how to use. Medicines form no part of a first aid kit, so, although you may carry medicines for your own use, you should not administer them to anyone else. This includes antiseptic creams, paracetamol, and burn creams.

The leader should carry a comprehensive first aid kit, but each member of the group should be able to cope with their own minor problems. The simplest first aid kit for personal use would probably consist of:

> waterproof plasters, various sizes – *to protect small cuts or blisters from infection (particularly from Weils Disease)*
>
> zinc oxide tape and scissors – *plasters by themselves on hands or fingers will quickly come off as they become wet. They can be secured by sticking a strip of zinc oxide tape over the plaster, taking it right around the finger, and then sticking down the end so that it overlaps onto itself. Keep checking that the tape has not been put on too tightly. If it has, the finger will tingle, or even turn blue as the circulation is cut off. The dressing must then immediately be retaped.*

Kayak Repair Kit

The leader of the group should be carrying a repair kit capable of coping with major repairs, eg the end of a kayak being knocked off. However, each member of the party should be able to cope with his or her own minor repairs, eg small holes and splits. As a minimum this might be a roll of single-sided carpet tape and an absorbent cloth to dry off the kayak so that the tape will stick. The cloth and tape need to be carried in a waterproof container. After applying the tape it is best to rub it hard. The friction will cause the tape to warm up and the "glue" then sticks much better.

It is very difficult to persuade tape to stick to a wet kayak in heavy rain ! An alternative is to use plumbers' tape. This will stick even if the kayak is wet, though it performs better if the boat is dried first. However, it also sticks to fingers and clothes, is difficult to cut, and is incredibly messy to handle ! It is therefore wise to pre-cut some lengths and then sandwich each length between two pieces of foil or thin plastic sheeting before folding down for storage.

Food and Drink

Take sufficient for any planned meal stop *plus* an extra ration of high calorie food in case you are delayed. Choose items which are easy to digest and will survive being bounced around in the back of a kayak. A couple of mars bars or their equivalent make ideal emergency rations. Food is easily tainted so pack your butties well away from the plumbers' tape if you want to enjoy them !

When it is cold, or you might be taking a few cold swims, consider taking a flask of something hot to drink. Metal unbreakable flasks are ideal but expensive. Plastic unbreakable flasks need to be pre-filled with boiling water if they are to stay hot for any length of time. Normal flasks can be protected by wrapping them in your spare clothing.

Dehydration can be a real problem in hot weather, so plenty of cold liquid needs to be carried. Avoid lemonade type drinks and crisps as the sugar and salt respectively will tend to dehydrate you further.

Waterproof Containers

The most readily available alternatives are:

Plastic Sweetie Jars
Most sweet shops will give their empty ones away to you but ask for them well in advance of your trip. The tops need to be taped on to make them watertight. Unfortunately they are not very robust and so must be checked before each trip.

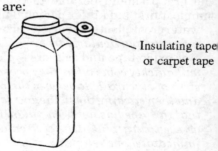 Insulating tape or carpet tape

BDH Containers
These can be purchased from most good kayak suppliers. They are very strong and will take a lot of punishment but are rarely completely watertight. A rubber collar (either specially purchased or cut off an appropriate sized car inner tube) around the lid join helps, but they still tend to take in a little moisture over a number of immersions. This leakage can be overcome by packing the contents inside good plastic containers

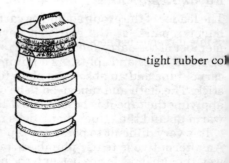 tight rubber col

inside the BDH. BDH containers are ideal for carrying such things as first aid kits, kayak repair kits and packed lunches – so long as you are not carrying plumbers' tape or resin as well !

Waterproof Sacks

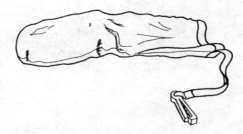

These can either be purchased from canoe suppliers, or neoprene backed nylon webbing straps and clips bought from various suppliers, and the sacks made up at home. The seams need to be taped to ensure the sack is watertight. This is achieved by sticking a strip of the neoprene backed nylon to the seamed area.

When stowing the sacks inside the kayak, care must be taken to avoid snagging the material on any sharp bolts or mends. Hard-edged containers inside the sack will also tend to rub through the material, so if any are carried they should be padded – eg wrapped up in some spare clothes.

Waterproof sacks, being fairly flexible, are ideal for carrying spare clothing. A piece of towelling or sponge placed near the neck of the sack will absorb any moisture that might come through the opening into the sack.

Any containers carried must be securely held inside the kayak either by elastics fibreglassed onto the inside of the boat or by being tied in. Any which are merely jammed in, no matter how tightly, will eventually be flushed out as a capsized and swamped kayak flexes in rough water.

Plastic Bivvy Bag

Highly recommended if canoeing in cold weather, not only for its value when exposure threatens, but, when wrapped around you, it also acts as a very effective windbreak for sitting having lunch on windswept river banks or shores. On sea trips, one opened out and held aloft makes you much more visible if rescue is needed. On no account let go of it if a helicopter is rescuing, as it could bring the aircraft down.

Torch

This can be very useful if your trip is likely to finish near sunset, especially during the winter when there is very little twilight. It is also worth packing if you are likely to explore any sea caves.

A waterproof torch is likely to survive a lot longer than a non-waterproof one.

Spare Paddles

If you have them, take them. A party should always carry at least one set of split paddles, particularly at sea.

Flares

For sea trips, the BCU recommends that as an absolute minimum, the party leader should carry two parachute flares and two hand-held flares and each member of the party should carry at least one hand held flare or other suitable means of attracting attention to one's location.

Flares need to be packed in totally watertight containers as any moisture soon renders them inoperable. An inexpensive but effective container can be made from a short length of plastic waste pipe. One end can be sealed by gluing onto it a plastic or PVC disc (use a waterproof glue !). A similar disc can be taped onto the other end. Care must be taken to ensure that not only does the tape make a watertight seal, but that the tape can be easily removed in the event of an emergency, by hands probably weakened by cold and fatigue.

Thought needs to be given as to where the flares are carried. Whether on the kayak or on the paddler, they must be secure and yet immediately accessible.

INDEX